Kids in Their Communities™

I Live at a Military Post

Stasia Ward Kehoe

The Rosen Publishing Group's
PowerKids Press™
New York

For Kevin, Thomas, and Mak

Published in 2000 by The Rosen Publishing Group, Inc.
29 East 21st Street, New York, NY 10010

First Edition

Book Design: Michael de Guzman

Photo Credits and Photo Illustrations: pp. 4, 8, 11, 12, 15, 16, 19, 20 by Paul Haring; p. 7 CORBIS/Bettmann

Kehoe, Stasia Ward, 1968–
     I live at a military post / Stasia Ward Kehoe.
         p. cm. —(Kids in their communities)
     Includes index.
     Summary: A third-grader describes what it is like living with his family on Fort Belvoir in Fairfax, Virginia.
     ISBN 0-8239-5441-2
     1. Fort Belvoir (Va.) Juvenile literature. 2. Children of military personnel—Virginia—Alexandria Juvenile literature. 3. United States. Army—Military life Juvenile literature. [1. Fort Belvoir (Va.) 2. United States. Army—Military life.] I. Title. II. Series: Kehoe, Stasia Ward, 1968– Kids in their communities.
UA26.F625K45   1999
355.7'09755'291—dc21   99-26370
                                                         CIP

Manufactured in the United States of America

CONTENTS

Michael

My name is Michael. I am nine years old. I live with my mom, stepdad, dog, and cat at an **army post** in Fairfax County, Virginia. The post is called Fort Belvoir. I have lived at Fort Belvoir for about a year. We moved here from Alaska, where my stepdad served a **tour of duty** at Fort Richardson.

Fort Belvoir is surrounded by beautiful plants and trees. There's plenty of room to play outside with my dog.

Beautiful to See

The Fort Belvoir land has an interesting history. It was once an English **estate**. In 1734, Thomas, the sixth Lord of Fairfax, asked his cousin Colonel William Fairfax to come and live in Virginia. William agreed to come to Virginia. He built a large home on Thomas's land. He called his home Belvoir, which means "beautiful to see." Young George Washington lived at nearby Mount Vernon. He often visited Belvoir.

Before George Washington became the first U.S. president, he was in the army. He visited Belvoir many times. ▶

Fort Belvoir's Mission

The Belvoir land became Fort Belvoir in 1935. From 1935 to 1989, Fort Belvoir was home to the army's **engineer** school. Today, there are 90 different groups **stationed** at Fort Belvoir. These groups include the U.S. Army **Intelligence** and **Security** Command, *Soldier's Magazine*, and divisions of the Army Reserve and National Guard. My stepdad says that Fort Belvoir's mission, or job, is to meet the needs of these important groups.

◀ *The soldiers at a military post work for the United States government.*

Communications Command

My stepfather is an army **sergeant**. He has an important job in **military communications**. Like many of the military men and women who live at Fort Belvoir, his work sometimes takes him off the post. Sometimes my stepdad gets to do work for the White House.

My family lives at a military post because my stepdad is an army sergeant. ▶

Woodlawn Village

Fort Belvoir is an important post. To me, it is also home. My family lives in the part of the post known as Woodlawn Village. Fourteen families live in my neighborhood. Someone from each family is a member of the military who has been stationed at Fort Belvoir. Family members who are not in the military are called **civilians**.

◀ *There are lots of other kids to play with in Woodlawn Village.*

School

Everyone in my school has a mom or a dad stationed at Fort Belvoir. Even though Fort Belvoir Elementary School is on the post's grounds, it is a part of the public school system of Fairfax County, Virginia. Fort Belvoir Elementary School is big and new. It was built because the post is growing. Fort Belvoir needed more classroom space for all the students who live here.

School is a good place for me to meet people when my family moves to a new post. ▶

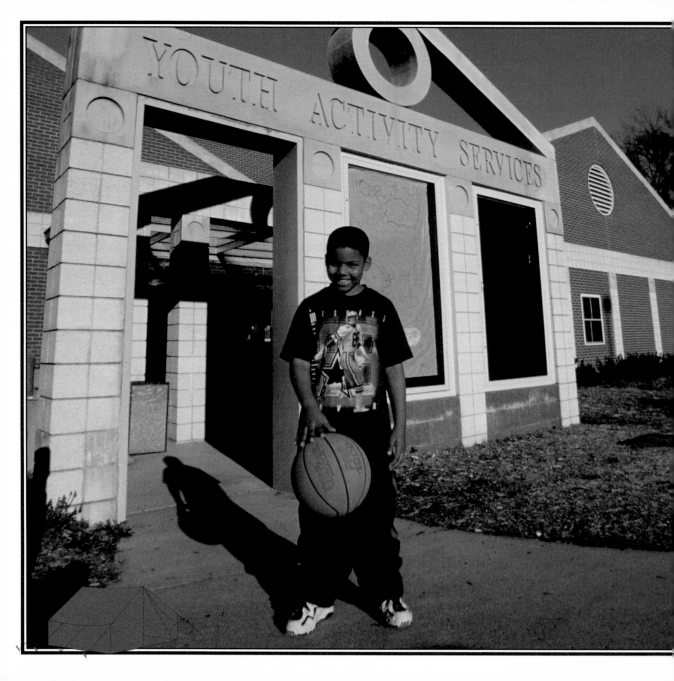

Community

After school, I like to go to the post's youth center. I can play Ping-Pong, pool, video games, and sports there. I like to play basketball. Fort Belvoir is so big that there are enough kids for six basketball teams at the youth center. My team is called the White Tigers. Besides the youth center, Fort Belvoir has its own community center, hospital, library, bank, churches, and a sports center. We even have a weekly newspaper, just for the people at the post. It is called the *Belvoir Eagle.*

◀ *I play basketball at the youth center.*

The Post Exchange

Shopping at the Post Exchange is lots of fun. The Post Exchange, which we call the PX, has lots of stores, so that military families can get everything they need without leaving the post. There is a **commissary**, where you can buy groceries, a video arcade, a big store called House and Garden, and, of course, a military clothing store. You can buy food, clothes, and furniture at the PX. You can also go to the PX to get your hair cut, your car repaired, or your laundry cleaned.

Whenever we need to buy something, my family goes to the Post Exchange. ▶

Rules

Like a town, a military post has car speed limits, recycling plans, and rules that everyone must follow. We even have our own police force, called the Military Police. One big difference between living on a military post and living in a regular town is that each person who works at a post has to carry an identification badge, or ID. The ID lets people know that you work at Fort Belvoir.

◀ *My stepdad keeps his ID with him when we go for a walk around the post.*

Military Life

Living at a military post is different from living in an ordinary town or city. Many people wear military uniforms. You need an identification badge to get around. Families come and go when their tour of duty, or job, at Fort Belvoir begins or ends. In other ways, a military post is like a regular town. It is a community where lots of people work together, or go to school together, and the things we need are nearby!